Design: Art of Design
Recipe Photography: Peter Barry
Jacket and Illustration Artwork: Jane Winton, courtesy
of Bernard Thornton Artists, London
Editors: Jillian Stewart and Kate Cranshaw

CLB 3530
Published by Grange Books, an imprint of Grange Books
PLC, The Grange, Grange Yard, London, SE1 3AG
© 1994 CLB Publishing, Godalming, Surrey, England.
Printed and bound in Singapore
Published 1994
ISBN 1-85627-459-4

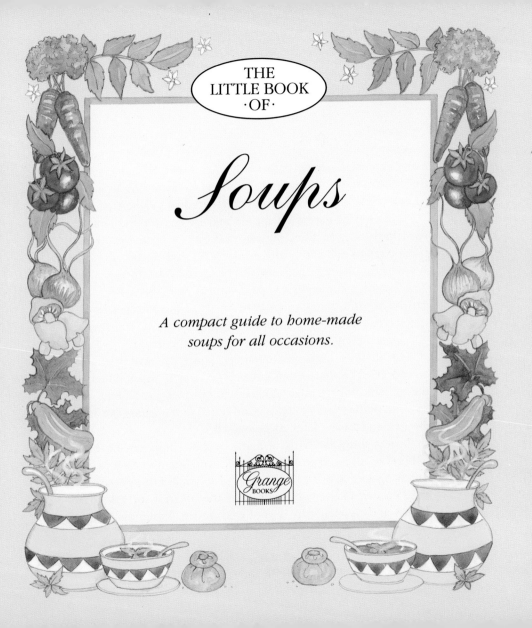

THE LITTLE BOOK ·OF·

Soups

*A compact guide to home-made
soups for all occasions.*

Grange
BOOKS

Introduction

Every country has soups included in its cuisine. Some Western speciality soups are only served in the smartest of establishments; others, particularly in the Far East, are served from roadside stalls from huge bubbling cauldrons. Both will be freshly made and both will probably be equally delicious.

Soups have a very wide appeal, and are enjoyed from infancy right into old age. They vary in consistency from the thinnest consommé to rich and hearty meal-in-one soups. Most soups are served steaming hot, but some can be sipped refreshingly chilled – perfect on a summer's day. Soups serve many occasions. They can be just the thing when you are short of time and need a quick meal, and they can make a delightful start to a meal when you want to linger with friends over several courses.

For all their tremendous variety, soups fall into two main categories. The first is the lighter type, which should stimulate the appetite for the main course without being too filling. The second, perhaps served with good bread and cheese, can make a quick and basic family meal in itself.

Broths form the basis of many soups. These can be based either on meat, vegetables or fish, and are themselves very satisfying to make. The boiling up of a handful of vegetables, a chicken carcass or ham bone, and the addition of a few bay leaves and peppercorns is very easy and will give the finished

soup a rounded, subtle flavour. The boiling of bones can be time-consuming, but with a pressure cooker it only takes 20 minutes. For convenience, the broth may be frozen for later use. And if making your own broth is inconvenient, then bouillon cubes are a tasty and convenient alternative.

Fine ingredients, such as fresh vegetables and herbs, a little wine or sherry, or some interesting spice such as ground coriander, make all the difference to quality when making soups.

Garnishes can alter the appearance of a soup. The aim should be to garnish soups with bright, contrasting colours and complementary flavours. Parsley is always popular for its vivid colour and fresh taste. Green onions and chives can be very successful substitutes for parsley, especially to give a welcome lift to the more bland creamy soups. Fresh basil is excellent in tomato-based soups, while grated Parmesan is delicious in moderation on thick, brown soups. A swirl of fresh or sour cream adds panache to the thicker pureed soups and looks more stylish still when topped with a sprinkling of fresh herbs or a spice such as paprika, cayenne, nutmeg or pepper.

Experiment with the appetising recipes in this book. Some are old favourites, while others are a little unusual – all are delicious and are sure to please both family and friends.

Dumpling Soup

SERVES 6-8

This is a Polish soup, the amount of dumplings can be altered to serve as a more filling meal, if wished.

PREPARATION: 25 mins
COOKING: 10 mins

1.5 litres/3 pints real beef stock

Filling
175g/6oz minced beef or pork
1 tsp chopped fresh marjoram
1 small onion, grated or very finely chopped
Salt and pepper

Dough
225g/8oz plain flour, sifted
Pinch salt
1-2 eggs
60ml/4 tbsps water

Chopped parsley

---

1. Combine all the filling ingredients, mixing very well.

2. Prepare the dough by sifting the flour with a pinch of salt into a large bowl. Make a well in the centre and add the eggs and water. Use only one egg if they are large.

3. Using a wooden spoon, beat the ingredients together, gradually incorporating flour until the

Step 6 Press the edges together to seal well and crimp with a fork.

dough becomes too stiff to beat.

4. Knead the dough until firm but elastic, then roll out very thinly on a floured surface and cut into 7.5cm/3-inch rounds

5. Place a small spoonful of filling on each circle and brush the edges with water.

6. Press the edges together to seal well, and crimp with a fork if wished.

7. Bring stock to the boil and add the dumplings. Cook about 10 minutes, or until all have floated to the surface.

8. Add some parsley to the soup, adjust the seasoning and serve in individual bowls or from a large tureen.

French Onion Soup

SERVES 4

This soup tastes best if cooked the day before it is needed and then reheated as required.

PREPARATION: 10 mins
COOKING: 45 mins

---

3 medium onions
60g/2oz butter or margarine
30g/1oz plain flour
1 litre/1¾ pints boiling real vegetable stock or
    water plus 2 stock cubes
Salt and pepper

Topping
4 slices French bread, cut crosswise
60g/2oz Cheddar cheese, grated
30g/1oz Parmesan cheese, grated

---

1. Slice the onions very finely into rings.

2. Melt the butter in a pan, add the onion rings and sauté over a medium heat until well browned.

3. Mix in the flour and stir well until browned.

4. Add the stock and seasoning and simmer for 30 minutes.

5. Toast the bread on both sides.

6. Combine both types of cheese, and divide between the bread slices. Place under a preheated medium grill, and toast until golden brown.

7. Place the slices of bread and cheese in the bottom of individual soup dishes and spoon the soup over the top. Serve at once.

Watercress Soup

SERVES 4

Watercress makes delicious soup, which can be served hot or cold, and is packed with vitamins too.

PREPARATION: 15 mins
COOKING: 45 mins

60g/2oz butter
1 leek, cleaned and thinly siced
225g/8oz potatoes, peeled and sliced thinly
570ml/1 pint chicken stock
Pinch grated nutmeg
Salt and freshly ground black pepper
4 good bunches of watercress, washed,
    trimmed and chopped
3 tbsps single cream
Few extra sprigs of watercress, for garnish

---

1. Melt the butter in a large saucepan and gently cook the leek until it is just soft, stirring frequently to prevent it from browning.

2. Add the potatoes, stock, nutmeg and

Step 1 Slowly soften the leek in the melted butter, stirring to prevent it from browning.

Step 3 Blend the soup in a food processor or liquidiser until the vegetables are very finely chopped.

seasoning to the saucepan. Bring to the boil, then cover and simmer for 15 minutes. Add the watercress and simmer for a further 10 minutes.

3. Cool the soup slightly, then using a food processor or blender, process until the vegetables are very finely chopped. Rinse the saucepan and stand a fine meshed nylon sieve over the cleaned pan.

4. Push the soup through the sieve using the back of a wooden spoon, until only the tough stalks remain and the soup in the pan is a fine purée.

5. Adjust the seasoning and stir the cream into the soup. Reheat gently, taking care not to boil it. Serve garnished with the reserved watercress sprigs and a little extra cream if wished.

Smoked Salmon Bisque

SERVES 6-8

You can buy bags of smoked salmon trimmings from supermarkets and delicatessens to use for this soup, if you have no leftovers.

PREPARATION: 10 mins
COOKING: 30 mins

Skin and trimmings of a side of smoked salmon
1 carrot
1-2 sticks of celery
1 onion, studded with cloves
Bay leaf
1 tsp salt
Few peppercorns
60g/2oz butter
60g/2oz plain flour
1 tbsp tomato purée
1 glass white wine or sherry
60ml/4 tbsps cream and 1 tbsp parsley, for
    garnishing

---

1. Put the smoked salmon skin and trimmings in a saucepan. Cut the carrot and celery into chunks. Add these to the pan along with the onion.

2. Cover with 1.4 litres/2 pints cold water, add the bay leaf, salt and peppercorns. Cover the pan and bring to the boil, then simmer for 20 minutes.

3. Remove the bay leaf. Take out the onion, remove the cloves and return the onion to the pan, chopped . With a spoon, remove the fish skin and scrape off any remaining flesh, which should also be returned to the pan. Strain half the liquid into a bowl.

4. In another large pan melt the butter, stir in the flour to make a roux and cook for 1 minute. Stir in the tomato purée and gradually add the strained stock, stirring constantly until it thickens. Add the wine or sherry.

5. Put the rest of the stock, containing the fish and vegetables, in a blender and run it for half a minute. Add this to the soup and season if necessary.

6. You can either stir the cream into the soup before serving or swirl a little on top of each bowl. Garnish with a little chopped parsley.

Indian Tomato Soup

SERVES 4

This highly fragrant and spicy tomato soup makes an interesting starter which is also low in calories.

PREPARATION: 15 mins
COOKING: 17-18 mins

225g/8oz tomatoes
2 tbsps vegetable oil
1 medium-sized onion, chopped
1 green chilli, seeded and finely chopped
3 cloves garlic, crushed
1 tbsp tomato purée
1 litre/1¾ pints water, or vegetable stock
4-6 curry leaves, or ½ tsp curry powder
Freshly ground sea salt, to taste
Coriander leaves and green chillies, for garnish

1. Cut a small cross in the skin of each tomato and plunge them into boiling water for 30-40 seconds.

2. Remove the tomatoes and carefully peel

Step 2 Remove the tomatoes from the boiling water and carefully peel away the loosened skin.

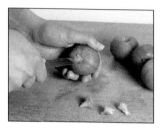

Step 2 Cut away and discard the hard green core from the tomatoes, and chop the flesh roughly with a sharp knife.

away the loosened skin with a sharp knife. Core and roughly chop the flesh.

3. Heat the oil in a large saucepan and gently sauté the onion, chilli and garlic for 3-4 minutes until soft, but not browned.

4. Stir in the tomatoes and cook for 5 minutes, stirring often to prevent the vegetables from burning.

5. Blend the tomato purée with the water and pour into the onions and tomatoes. Add the curry leaves or powder, season with the salt and simmer for 5-7 minutes.

6. Remove the soup from the heat and stir in the coriander leaves and the chilli halves.

7. Pour the soup into 4-6 serving bowls and serve piping hot, discarding the chilli garnish before eating.

Sweet Potato Soup

SERVES 4-6

Warm up your winter days with this hearty soup.

PREPARATION: 15 mins
COOKING: 40-55 mins

60g/2oz butter or margarine
1 large onion, finely chopped
460g/1lb sweet potato, peeled and diced
225g/8oz carrots, peeled and diced
1 tbsp chopped fresh coriander
Grated zest and juice of 1 lemon
850ml/1½ pints stock
Pepper

---

1. Melt the butter or margarine in a large saucepan, add the onion and cook until transparent.

2. Add the sweet potato and carrots and allow to 'sweat' over a very low heat for 10-15 minutes, stirring occasionally.

3. Add the coriander, lemon zest, juice of half the lemon, the stock and pepper. Cover and simmer for 30-40 minutes.

4. Liquidise the soup in a blender or food processor until almost smooth, but leaving some texture to the soup.

5. Return to the pan and reheat until piping hot. Garnish with coriander leaves and serve immediately.

Wonton Soup

SERVES 6-8

Probably the best-known Chinese soup, this recipe uses pre-made wonton wrappers for ease of preparation.

PREPARATION: 25-30 mins
COOKING: 5-10 mins

90g/3oz finely minced chicken or pork
2 tbsps chopped fresh coriander
3 spring onions, finely chopped
2.5cm/1-inch piece fresh root ginger, peeled
  and grated
20-24 wonton wrappers
1 egg, lightly beaten
1.4 litres/2½ pints real chicken stock
1 tbsp dark soy sauce
Dash sesame oil
Salt and pepper
Coriander or watercress, to garnish

---

1. Mix together the chicken or pork, coriander, spring onions and ginger. Place all the wonton wrappers on a large, flat surface. Brush the edges of the wrappers lightly with beaten egg.

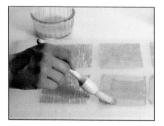

Step 1 Place the wonton wrappers out on a clean surface. Brush edges with beaten egg.

Step 2 Place a spoonful of filling on half of each wrapper

2. Place a small mound of the meat mixture on each of the wrappers and fold the other half over the top to form a triangle. Press with the fingers to seal the edges well.

3. Bring the stock to the boil in a large saucepan. Add the filled wontons and simmer for 5-10 minutes or until they float to the surface. Add the remaining ingredients to the soup, using only the leaves of the coriander or watercress for garnish.

Step 2 Fold over the tops and press firmly with the fingers to seal.

Fennel and Walnut Soup

SERVES 4

A delicious and unusual combination makes this soup perfect for special occasions.

PREPARATION: 15 mins
COOKING: 1 hr

---

1 bulb fennel
1 head celery
1 tbsp olive or sunflower oil
1 large onion, chopped
90g/3oz walnuts, crushed
1.14 litres/2 pints vegetable stock, bean stock or
    water
3 tbsps Pernod
140ml/¼ pint single cream
Salt and pepper
Parsley, to garnish

---

1. Chop the fennel and celery into small chunks. Heat the oil over a low heat in a saucepan and sauté the fennel and celery with the onion for 20-30 minutes.

2. Add the walnuts and stock and simmer for 30 minutes.

3. Liquidise the simmered ingredients in a blender or food processor and return to the pan.

4. Add the Pernod, single cream and salt and pepper.

5. Reheat gently without boiling and serve garnished with chopped parsley.

Hot and Sour Soup

SERVES 4-6

This very warming soup is a winter favourite in China. Add the chilli sauce and vinegar to suit your taste.

PREPARATION: 25 mins
COOKING: 7-8 mins

60g/2oz pork
60g/2oz peeled, uncooked prawns
1.4 litres/2½ pints real chicken stock
3 dried Chinese mushrooms, soaked in boiling
    water for 5 minutes, chopped
30g/1oz bamboo shoots, sliced
3 spring onions, shredded
Salt and pepper
1 tbsp sugar
1 tsp dark soy sauce
½ tsp light soy sauce
1-2 tsps chilli sauce
1½ tbsps vinegar
Dash sesame oil and rice wine or sherry
1 egg, well beaten
2 tbsps water mixed with 1 tbsp cornflour

Soak the dried mushrooms in boiling water for 5 minutes.

Step 3 Pour the egg into the hot soup and stir gently to form threads.

1. Trim any fat from the pork and slice it into shreds about 5cm/2 inches long and less than 5mm/¼-inch thick.

2. Place the pork in a large saucepan with the prawns and stock. Bring to the boil and then reduce the heat to allow to simmer gently for 4-5 minutes. Add all the remaining ingredients except for the egg and the cornflour and water mixture. Cook a further 1-2 minutes over low heat.

3. Remove the pan from the heat and add the egg gradually, stirring gently until it forms threads in the soup.

4. Mix a spoonful of the hot soup with the cornflour and water mixture and add to the soup, stirring constantly.

5. Bring the soup back to simmering point for 1 minute to thicken the cornflour. Serve immediately.

Rich Brown Soup

SERVES 4

Use real beef stock as the basis of this soup.

PREPARATION: 30 mins
COOKING: 2 hrs

60g/2oz butter or margarine
75g/2½oz flour
700ml/1¼ pints water
420ml/¾ pint beef stock
Salt and pepper
Dash Worcestershire sauce
Grated cheese
Fresh parsley, to garnish

1. Heat the butter or margarine in a large pot until melted. Stir in the flour, then cook over a low heat, stirring constantly, until the flour is a rich brown colour.

2. Gradually stir in the water and stock. Stir constantly while adding the liquid to prevent lumps from forming.

3. Add some salt and pepper and Worcestershire sauce. Cover the pot and simmer slowly for about 2 hours to fully develop the flavour.

4. Serve sprinkled with grated cheese and garnished with parsley.

Courgette Soup with Lemon

SERVES 4-6

The fresh taste of lemon and courgettes makes this a delicious soup which can be served either hot or cold.

PREPARATION: 20 mins
COOKING: 25 mins

---

1 medium onion, thinly sliced
2 tbsps olive oil
460g/1lb courgettes, topped, tailed and sliced
Finely grated rind and juice of 1 large lemon
420ml/¾ pint chicken stock
Freshly ground black pepper
2 egg yolks
200ml/7 fl oz natural yogurt

---

1. In a large pan, sauté the onion gently in the olive oil for 3 minutes until it is just transparent. Add the courgettes and cook for a further 2-3 minutes.

2. Stir in all remaining ingredients except the egg yolks and yogurt, cover and simmer for 20 minutes.

Step 3 Blend the soup in a liquidiser, or food processor, until it is smooth.

3. Transfer the soup to a liquidiser or food processor, and blend until smooth.

4. Mix the egg yolks into the yogurt and stir into the blended soup. Reheat the soup gently, stirring all the time until it thickens. Do not allow the soup to boil.

5. Serve hot at this stage, or transfer to a refrigerator and chill thoroughly.

Step 1 In a large pan gently sauté the onion until it is just transparent.

Step 4 Mix together the egg yolks and yogurt in a small jug or bowl.

Spicy Chilli Bean Soup

SERVES 4-6

This 'complete meal' soup is full of flavour, and is ideal for a cold day.

PREPARATION: 30 mins
COOKING: 1 hr

---

3 tbsps vegetable oil
2 onions, roughly chopped
1 clove garlic, crushed
1 tbsp ground cumin
2 tsps paprika
1 red or green chilli, seeded and finely
    chopped
225g/8oz minced beef
800g/1¾lbs canned tomatoes, chopped
850ml/1½ pints chicken or vegetable stock
90g/3oz tomato purée
1 tsp oregano
1 bay leaf
140ml/¼ pint beer
Freshly ground black pepper
120g/4oz each of canned red kidney beans,
    chick peas, and white pinto beans, drained
    and thoroughly rinsed.

---

1. Heat the oil in a large, heavy-based saucepan. Add the onions and garlic and cook slowly until they become transparent.

2. Stir in the cumin, paprika and chilli.

Step 6 Add the drained beans to the soup during the last 15 minutes of cooking time.

Increase the heat and cook quickly for 30 seconds, stirring all the time.

3. Add the meat and cook until lightly browned, breaking up any large pieces with a fork.

4. Add the tomatoes and their juice, the stock, tomato purée, oregano, bay leaf, beer and ground pepper. Stir well, then bring to the boil.

5. Cover and simmer for about 50 minutes, checking the level of liquid several times during cooking and adding more water if needed.

6. During the last 15 minutes of cooking, add the drained beans, stirring them in to mix well.

Turkey Chowder

SERVES 6-8

Serve this good filling soup with crusty bread for a meal in itself.

PREPARATION: 15 mins
COOKING: 3½ hrs

Turkey bones
1 bay leaf
3 black peppercorns
1 blade of mace
1 onion, unpeeled
200g/7oz pearl barley, rinsed
3 stalks celery, sliced
3 carrots, diced
175g/6oz green beans, sliced
150g/5oz canned sweetcorn, drained
2 tbsps chopped parsley

---

1. Use the carcass from a roast turkey. Break up the carcass and place in a large pot with any skin and leftover meat, the bay leaf, peppercorns, mace and onion.

2. Pour in 2.3 litres/4 pints cold water to cover the bones, and then cover the pot. Bring to the boil, then simmer, partially covered, for about 2 hours.

3. Strain and reserve the stock. Remove any meat from the bones, dice and reserve.

4. Combine the strained stock, barley, celery, carrots and green beans. Partially cover and bring to the boil, then reduce the heat and simmer for 1-1½ hrs, or until the barley is tender. Add the corn after about 45 minutes cooking time, and stir in the chopped parsley and any diced turkey.

Egg and Lemon Soup

This is one of the best known of all Greek soups. Diced chicken can be added to make it more filling if wished.

PREPARATION: 15 mins
COOKING: 15 mins

1.4 litres/2½ pints real chicken stock
60g/2oz rice, rinsed
2 eggs, beaten
Juice of 2 lemons

1. Bring the stock to the boil in a large saucepan. When boiling, add the rice and cook for about 10 minutes.

2. Meanwhile, beat the eggs with 1 tbsp cold water for about 3 minutes, or until lightly frothy. Add the lemon juice and beat for about 1 minute to blend well.

Step 2 Add the lemon juice to the eggs, straining out any pips. Beat for about a minute to blend well.

Step 3 Beat a few spoonfuls of the hot stock into the egg mixture.

3. Beat a few spoonfuls of the hot stock into the egg mixture. Gradually add back to the pan, stirring continuously. Put the soup back over a very low heat for about 1-2 minutes, stirring constantly. Do not allow the soup to boil. Serve immediately.

Step 3 Pour the egg mixture back into the stock in a thin, steady stream, stirring continuously. Do not allow to boil.

Wild Rice Soup

SERVES 4

A meal in itself when served with granary bread and a green salad.

PREPARATION: 15 mins
COOKING: 50 mins

60g/2oz wild rice
420ml/¾ pint water
2 onions, chopped
15g/½oz butter or ghee
2 sticks celery, chopped
½ tsp dried thyme
½ tsp dried sage
850ml/1½ pints vegetable stock
1 tbsp soy sauce
6 small potatoes, peeled and roughly chopped
1 carrot, finely diced
Milk or single cream

---

1. Add the wild rice to the water, bring to the boil, reduce the heat and simmer for 40-50 minutes until the rice has puffed and most of the liquid has been absorbed.

2. Meanwhile, in a saucepan sauté the onions in the butter until transparent. Add the celery, thyme and sage and cook for 5-10 minutes.

3. Add the stock, soy sauce and potatoes. Simmer for about 20 minutes or until the potatoes are tender.

4. Blend the mixture in a liquidiser until smooth. Return to the pan, add the carrot and wild rice.

5. Add some milk or cream to thin the soup to the desired consistency. Reheat gently, without boiling, and serve.

Lentil Soup with Sausage

SERVES 6-8

**This German soup includes bratwurst which helps make this hearty enough
for a meal in itself.**

PREPARATION: 15 mins, plus 3-4 hrs soaking
COOKING: 1½ hrs

340g/12oz brown or Egyptian lentils, well
  washed
120g/4oz streaky bacon, derinded and
  chopped
1 onion, thinly sliced
4 sticks celery, sliced
2 carrots, peeled and thinly sliced
45g/1½oz butter or margarine
3-4 bratwurst, cut into 2.5cm/1-inch pieces
1 tbsp flour
280ml/½ pint water or stock
2 tsps wine vinegar
Salt and pepper

1. Soak the lentils in enough water to cover, for
3-4 hours. Drain and place in a large stock pot.

Step 1 Once
lentils have
cooked for
about 20
minutes, scum
may rise to the
surface. Skim
this off as the
soup cooks.

Step 2 Whisk
the water or
stock into the
flour gradually
to prevent
lumps forming.

Add the bacon, onion, celery, carrots and 1
litre/1¾ pints water. Bring to the boil, cover and
simmer for 45 minutes.

2. When lentils are almost cooked, melt the
butter in a frying pan and fry the bratwurst until
brown. Remove and set aside. Stir the flour into
the butter in the pan and gradually whisk in the
additional water or stock. Bring to the boil,
stirring continuously. Add the vinegar and
seasonings and allow to boil for about 1
minute.

3. Stir the mixture into the soup, blending
thoroughly. Bring back to the boil and then
allow the soup to simmer, uncovered, for a
further 40-50 minutes, or until the lentils are
completely tender. Add the bratwurst and heat
through.

Carrot Soup

SERVES 4

Carrots make a most delicious soup which is both filling and quick to prepare.

PREPARATION: 12 mins
COOKING: 25 mins

460g/1lb carrots
1 medium onion
1 medium turnip
2 cloves garlic, crushed
700ml/1¼ pints water or vegetable stock
½ tsp dried thyme
½ tsp ground nutmeg
Salt and ground white pepper, to taste
Toasted sunflower seeds, flaked almonds and
    pistachio nuts, mixed together for garnish

---

1. Peel the carrots and cut them into thick slices. Peel and roughly chop the onion and turnip.

2. Put the vegetables, garlic and water or stock, into a large saucepan and bring to the boil.

Step 1 Using a sharp knife, roughly chop the peeled onions and turnip.

Cover the pan, reduce the heat and simmer for 20 minutes.

3. Add the herbs and seasoning, and simmer for a further 5 minutes.

4. Using a liquidiser or food processor, blend the soup until it is thick and smooth.

5. Reheat the soup as required, garnishing with the seeds and nuts before serving.

Step 1 Cut the carrots into thick slices, approximately 1.25cm/½-inch thick.

Step 4 Purée the soup in a liquidiser or food processor, until it is thick and smooth.

Split Pea Soup

SERVES 4-6

The ham bone adds lots of flavour to this thick hearty soup.

PREPARATION: 10 minutes, plus overnight soaking
COOKING: 1-1¼ hrs

460g/1lb split peas
1 ham bone
1 small onion, finely chopped
1 bay leaf
45g/1½oz butter
3 tbsps flour
Salt and pepper
420ml/¾ pint milk
Chopped fresh mint, or other herbs
Croutons

1. Soak the peas overnight in enough water to cover. Drain, then place in a large saucepan with 1.4 litres/2½ pints of cold water along with the ham bone, onion and bay leaf.

2. Bring to the boil, then simmer for 45-50 minutes until the peas are very tender. Remove the ham bone, cut off any meat and chop it into small pieces.

3. Remove the bay leaf and purée the soup, if wished, and return the meat to the soup.

4. Melt the butter in a large pan and stir in the flour until smooth and well blended. Cook for 1 minute, add salt and pepper and gradually stir in the milk.

5. Cook, stirring constantly until thickened. Add the split pea mixture and cook until very thick.

6. Add some chopped mint. Serve with croutons and extra mint.

Index

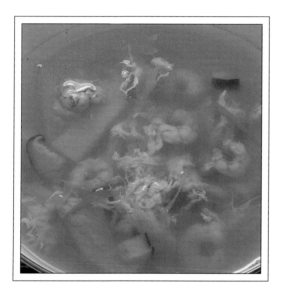